COCO ISLAND

Christine Roseeta Walker is a Jamaican poet and novelist living on the outskirts of Manchester, England. She studied Creative Writing at the University of Salford and the University of Manchester. Her debut novel, *The Grass is Weeping*, is a revenge tragedy set in Jamaica. She also works as a commissioned poet with an archaeologist working in the Peak District, and she spends her time writing and organising poetry reading workshops in care homes for people living with dementia.

Coco Island
Christine Roseeta Walker

CARCANET POETRY

First published in Great Britain in 2024 by
Carcanet
Alliance House, 30 Cross Street
Manchester, M2 7AQ
www.carcanet.co.uk

A CIP catalogue record for this book is
available from the British Library.

ISBN 978 1 80017 400 9

Book design by Andrew Latimer, Carcanet
Typesetting by LiteBook Prepress Services

The publisher acknowledges financial
assistance from Arts Council England.

CONTENTS

ONE

TWO

THREE

FOUR

FIVE

SIX

SEVEN

For
Winston Washington
Walker

COCO ISLAND

ONE

COCO ISLAND

From behind the bottle tree, a red sun rises,
shifting colours of pink, orange, and yellow
onto the sand and out into the sea.

From daybreak to nightfall, the Island waits.
Sea-bound, knee-deep in waters too vast
to allow bridges to form between cays.

Each day, glass-bottom boats part waves
to unload the weight of them that come
to dine and dance beneath the bottle tree.

From zinc pits, the scent of meat burning
rises above easy reggae music and euphoric voices
as idle waves lap at the golden sands.

Beneath the bottle tree, they fall in love
with the blue sea and the blue sky blurring,
while the sun turns the evening blood-orange.

But the Island is listening, observing every
gesticulation and conduct until It identifies
them by their attentiveness.

When the Island had hosted them beneath
the bottle tree, they climbed back onto the boats,
delighted to have come to Coco Island.

But often, on the journey back, a sacrifice
must be made — a human offering must be given,
for the Island, too, must feed to survive.

This is the law of paradise: something taken
for something given. It is Coco Island's nature —
a muted transaction since its creation.

So, if you should come to Coco Island,
never dance beneath the bottle tree or behave
inattentively: The Island is watching.

BLACK SHEEP

Dusk was near, but not nearby enough
for you to miss your way
onto our verandah.

White dress and hair cut like a man's,
you sat with your legs wide
squinting into the fading light.

Two strangers we were, each one pretending
to know the other — mother, daughter —
daughter, mother, yet unfamiliar.

The black frock you brought was a funeral dress
puffing out at the hems with layers and layers
of black web… webbing

black with mesh netting to wrap
me in… to haul me away in that giant black bag
nesting at your restless heel.

I look at you without thought
like I did on the last Sabbath day I saw you stumbling
down that slippery slope.

When my father stood with me at the front door,
he said that I was the black sheep —
the black sheep… in your eyes.

And now, on this verandah with the black night
crawling in, all thought escapes me as I gaze
into your blue eyes — who are you?

What were your excuses, then? Ends meet —
you had left to make ends meet, and now you have returned
holding the ends of a severed circle.

You carried the empty bag to my bedroom in silence,
ate quietly at my brother's table and listened
as I read from a pile of textbooks.

The small double bed sinking under our weight
as we slip the thin cotton sheet over our feet.
You never talked of those lost years

or said why you had come or why you had with you
that empty bag. At daylight, when the rooster crowed thrice
I awoke from my sleep, you were gone.

A dead-ended telephone number fell off the pillow
onto the floor. I perceive the scourge
in me that had driven you away once more.

Years after my father had died, I saw you again.
But you had gotten smaller. Your blue
eyes were even bluer, still unfamiliar.

At dusk, I listened to you talk on the hotel balcony
and waited quietly for something visceral to happen —
for some pull to guide me.

It was on that night when the light from the moon
had flooded the mango tree that I saw a black shape
sitting in your seat.

THE HOUSE

It's the daylight darkness he remembers the most,
the windowless rooms and the rays of grey beams fighting
to float through the twisted stick walls.

     He could never find anything in that black house.
But each time he thinks of the darkness, he sees his father
pulling at the end of the galvanised chain holding him to the wall.

     The chains were secured in the mornings; his metal mother
chiding him with sharp clinking to stop him straying,
and were removed at night while he watched for empathy.

     One morning, he searched the darkness and found the key
to freedom. After work, his worn father caught him
with the neighbours' kids. The key disappeared for good.

     Then, it was just the darkness, the weight of metal
scarfing his neck and the solemn vows to himself
of leaving once he was old enough to depart.

     Years later, as he watched his only son playing
with the neighbours' children, he thought of his father,
trying to understand his lasting cruelty.

     At times, he finds himself drawn to the darkness
inside his scarred mind, and to resist, he paints
giant windows on his walls to let the light in.

LIKE BUFFALOS

That sweltering June day on the bridge
above the molasses waters of the Negril River
we saw him half-naked and vulnerable.

Passers-by had stopped to watch him
convulse involuntarily towards the riverbank
while hazarding a guess to his ailment.

Spasming, rolling, frothing at the mouth
and moving closer to the water's pebbled edge,
he had no control of his defeated limbs.

We watched his body fall, rise, fall
thinking of a hundred ways to help, but knowing
we were too weak, too small to pull him back.

The adults looked numbed, petrified,
saying he might grab hold of them if they try
to stop him falling into the glossy marsh.

Our uncle signalled it was time to go
before the stranger rolled down the riverbank,
and plunged into the moving current.

We walked away, trying not to look back,
hearing our uncle's guttural voice explaining
how quick it takes a human to drown.

If only people were like buffalos,
it would take him hours before his lungs failed
and enough time to get help, he said.

The stranger had vanished behind
the crowd as we crossed the road to the market,
hoping the murky waters would revive him.

TWO

Above the logwood trees, where
blue skies linger all day, my father
still sees you shining
in the heat. Your twin sister stand-
ing beside you with titanium steel
as you both
glare down on the town from your
concrete splints behind a green-
wired fence.
How the years have slipped by since
my father
dug the dirt trenches past the
crowded graveyard, where duppies
play at midday
and desert at midnight until he
reached the white hill where you
grew, busting out of red clay and
tree roots with large smooth edges,
curving your magnificent bodies.
Two useless giants, visible, and still
are, from every street corner, shiny,
elegant,
pride of place on a hill the residents
now call by your names. On the day
of your baptism, my father rushed
from the house, carrying buckets up
to the fence where the community

had gathered to watch you both
wash the embankment, the bucket
and the hands that held them away.
The force of your waters raged for
hours until the neighbours stumbled
down the sodden hill, optimistic
that this was your inauguration, you
making yourselves ready to serve
the community. But the years faded,
and you never woke again, not even
during the worst droughts. Later,
when the rain came, the narrow
dirt lane expanded into our gardens,
exposing those useless iron veins
laid so many years before you were
even aimlessly inhabiting those
scorching plinths.
Now, my father sits beneath his
ackee tree, recalling the hours he
had spent
bending in those trenches, digging out
large rocks with men like him who
had thought you were their pride
and their deliverer. But you were
never built
to give us life, only the emptiness of
believing.

DRUNK CHAPERONE

We walked towards the party under a sky of stars
trying not to sway beyond a straight line
like he was. Our uncle, tour guide, tipsy chaperone
swore to show us, children, how to navigate
the night town.

We followed him, three girls, up a hill until we reached
the celebration, confetti floating in the hotel pool.
They served us soda and told us to sit wherever we wanted
while our guide drank rum and coke and quarrelled
with the host.

Minutes later, we followed the curving concrete wall
until we came to the town centre, the sea air raw
on our deflated faces as we climbed the local cinema steps.
Our uncle cajoled the man at the door until he let us in
free of charge.

As we sat down in the dark and crowded picture room,
he stood up, pointed at the screen and shouted,
"disgusting! This show is inappropriate for young children!"
The crowd murmured as we pushed our way
to the door.

Downstairs, he slurred, "What you like fi do now?
We girls glanced at each other and said, "Home."
He staggered ahead for a moment, then began searching
his pockets for cigarettes. He stopped and glanced up
at the sky.

"You know what this means?" he asked." You will have to go
home without me." We let out a soft cry,
scared to walk the darkened streets so close to midnight.
But before we could protest, our chaperone
had left us.

We began bracing ourselves, afraid to trust all shadows,
when we saw Granny waving her arms in the air.
She led us back the straight way, swearing to curse bad words.
When he came to ask if we'd made it home, Granny
answered no.

We could hear him all night going up and down the veranda
steps calling our names and shouting to our granny
to check the bedrooms. At daylight, we found him asleep
on the concrete floor, piled by his feet, his broken
cigarettes.

THE YELLOW INFLATABLE

And so, the yellow inflatable drifted.
Me, up to my waist, wading, trying
to reach the raft as the children churn
water into salt, and I was overwhelmed.

And so, I tripped beneath the waves
where the shallow became deep,
where sea turned blindingly bright,
and where all fight and fear fled.

And so, the yellow inflatable drifted.
The shrill cries of excitement muted,
as I floated away, slipping from
this sphere through a vortex to the next.

And so, I rode the shimmering waves
till my brother's foraging hands
pierced the brightness
and pulled me above the saline surface.

And so, the yellow inflatable drifted
even when we reached home and our father
got upset that we had gone swimming without
leave; I was adrift on the yellow inflatable.

THREE

THE SLOW ONES

When her family was asleep, Celia
liked standing by the window watching
the moonless darkness by lamplight.
Her mind's eye glowed low in a world
so still it made her head grow large.
For a while, she would glimpse them,
white-laced and slowly marching
past her quiet house.

      Twice, she called out to them and asked
      why they march, but tomb-like silence,
      was their manner, till a night
      one came, pausing at the window,
      and gave her an icy lantern
      with its face pointing the wrong way,
      then gliding backwards to re-join
      the slow marching ones.

            When day came, her father observed
            the lantern burning emerald flame
            and gave her rosemary water
            to wash herself while her mother
            went hunting a new-born baby
            and its mummy to spend the night,
            else the lantern would ferry her
            across that same night.

Twice, the emerald fire flickered
but the slow ones did not appear
not until the house was sound dead.
Celia stood by the window
holding the baby in one hand
and the lantern in the other,
she watched their white-laced attire
shuffling closer.

> When a hand reached out to take hers
> she tickled the baby awake
> and made it cry for sleep again.
> The hand withdrew, and the lantern
> glided away from the window
> until it was back in the line.
> Celia said that was the first time
> she had seen the dead.

BRANDY BEFORE BED

Faye's grandmother was a brandy lover.
Each night, an hour before bed,
She would send a reluctant Faye
to the shops to buy a drink of brandy.

It was always at half past nine, so close
to midnight when moonlit shadows
darkened the path to the main road
and her slow uncle never walked behind.

Faye would watch the shopkeeper measuring
the drink in a glass flask before
pouring it into a clear cup,
while she rubbed her palms to cover the rim.

Back home, the drink was left on the nightstand
and covered with a greeting card
to prevent the strength from fading,
from flatlining in the tranquil back room.

When it was time for bed, Faye's grandmother
filled the brandy cup with water
and drank it down, leaving an inch
in the bottom, which she offered to Faye.

Faye never understood why her granny
enjoyed a weak drink before bed
or how she had lived a century
sipping such insipidness as brandy.

RED LEATHER BAG

My father is chasing the bus again
through the town square
under the heat of the noonday sun.

The drowsy driver had driven off
with our red leather bag
before he could free it from the trunk.

My father is pounding on the windows
his khaki trousers brushing
recklessly against the back wheel.

The bus halts at the roundabout
where the local All Age School
planted a tropical garden for calm.

My father is walking back
wet, worn out, panting,
but proudly carrying our leather bag.

The bus clears the roundabout
and makes its final stop
at the bus station across the road.

IT'S NOW UP TO YOU, SORRY

I'm apologising again, sorry.
So, it has been six months? Sorry.
So, you have been sleeping rough? Sorry.
So, you have been in jail? Sorry.
For nearly... how long? For nearly a year? Sorry.
For breaking your thieving sister's windows? Sorry.
For shouting out in the courthouse? Sorry.
You need another psychiatric evaluation? Sorry.
You need a new address when you come out? Sorry.
You can't use the toilet when you want to? Sorry.
I'm getting the best lawyer I can afford, sorry.
I'm apologising again, sorry.
I'm still waiting to sign the bail bond, sorry.
It's a shame you can't go back to your home, sorry.
It's a long way to your new house, sorry.
You don't like the way the town looks? Sorry.
You feel we're leaving you there to die? Sorry.
You hate the headstones near the house? Sorry.
The people living on the hill are all ugly? Sorry.
The temperature this high is too cold? Sorry.
The house you're living in is haunted? Sorry.
You can't get the shows you like? Sorry.
You think working the land is tough? Sorry.
You can't spend another night? Sorry.
I'm apologising again, sorry.
I don't know what else to do, sorry
it's now up to you, sorry.

THE FALLEN CHRIST

While all the town was quiet, we sat below the starry sky
to the inclining sound of our father's voice,
when the shy willow became his nightly stage, a past forgotten,
found, and lived for one moment again.
As we listened to the tale of our father falling into a river
a bright light illuminated the willow.
We saw a fireball passing above the transfigured tree.
Its presence was so near we felt its warmth inside our hearts
and saw our father going down the darkened hill.
Gone for imagined hours,
we held our position beneath the willow tree
until he returned, muted by the flame.
When he spoke the next day, he said he had seen the Christ,
standing in a ring of light
with bloodstained palms and hair matted into dreads.
The fallen Christ had commanded him
to give up meat, to take the Nazarite vow, and follow Him.
From then, our father ate only Ital stews
and grew his hair until his face and his past-past disappeared.
Years later, when his sight began to fail,
and his hair was nearly touching the ground, we asked him
what did he really see in the fallen light that night?
He answered, "The hand of Jah pulling me from the river."

FOUR

BLUE LACE DRESS

Once upon a time, there were two cousins -
two little girls living on the same family land.
One had a lot, and the other had very little.
The one who had much lived with her mother
and father. She had her own bedroom, new toys
and beautiful dresses.
The one with very little lived with her great aunt.
She knew no father or mother and never got toys
or beautiful things except hairclips.
Her bedroom was a corner in her aunt's room.
The two girls spent hours playing on the lawn,
none thinking the other better.
The mother with a lot would borrow anything
the child with little had that looked pretty enough.
She would borrow the hairclips of the one with little
and adorned her daughter's hair with white, red
blue and yellow bows, daisy and heart shape snaps,
only returning them on request.
The child with little never complained. She loved
her cousin and never felt the need to resent her.
But, one day, the entire family was invited to a grand wedding
at a lighthouse. The aunt of the child with little wanted
to make a good impression for the groom was a distant
cousin – a man worthy of honour.
The aunt decided to buy the child with little a new
dress, the first dress she would wear
that was brand new. The dress was being sold
by a neighbour whose daughter never wore
it to a cancelled wedding that eluded them.
The child with little aunt agreed to pay
for the dress in stages and took the child to fit

it on the neighbour's veranda, blue lace
and satin tulle that swept the floor when turning.
The child with little took the dress home on a rack.
Everyone saw the dress that day and paid her
compliments, saying she would be pretty as plum.
The girl with a lot came and said her mother
would buy her a yellow dress as pretty as the sun.
The child with little felt something heating up
inside her for the first time.
The mother of the child with much went to the neighbour
the next day and asked to buy the dress,
offering to pay good money upfront.
The neighbour said the dress was already sold
and that she would need to buy it from the new owner.
The mother came to the aunt's house and asked
to borrow the dress, saying the child with little
could wear one of her daughter's dresses
since her daughter had grown a little chubby recently
and nothing inside their huge wardrobe fitted.
The aunt rolled her eyes, then told her to go to hell,
where the Devil and his archangels were waiting
for covetous people like her to poke with His red-hot
fork for all eternity.
The child with little, heard her aunt calling down
curses on the mother with a lot and felt secure;
her aunt would keep the blue dress safe for her.
On the day of the wedding, the child with a lot wore
a yellow dress without lace, and sat under the marquee,
at the same table, watching their distant cousin marrying
his bride, as the sun settled on the blue sea.
The yellow coronations decorating the white table
looked brighter than her cousin's dress
as the groom introduced his new American bride.
The mother with a lot shuffled awkwardly in her seat

while the groom danced with the girl who had little.
When the reception was over, the child with a lot
said to the child with little that she never wanted
to take her blue dress, and that it was her mother's wish
to keep them apart.
The next day, they played together in secret,
and so began the counting down of years until they were old
enough to care about blue lace dresses.

THE YOUNG BULLFIGHTER

Four cloven hooves, four thin sandals echoing
behind and then ahead on the dirt track.
The red clay was like a matador's cape,
soft, bright and inescapable.

Brave adults scaled barbed wire fences,
ran in the opposite directions and skipped
up maroon concrete steps into a crowded,
frantic shop.

The urgent voice of a man shouting,
'get off the road!' but there was no place to go.
The lane ahead suddenly bent behind a tall
dark-heartwood and cerasee bush hedge,

Her brother would not stop.
They were on their way to visit their father
at work with his lunch basket.
Four cloven hooves, they saw them black with fur

which climbed up knobby knees and neck,
then vanished. He dropped his basket
and nudged her into the nearest edging.
He stood in front of her, inflexible.

They could hear the farmer's voice calling,
"get out the way, mad bull, mad bull!"
She watched from below his elbow
as the bull charged at them.

Its eyes mean and gaping, its nostrils flaring,
its mouth huge and breath heavy.
Her brother, only ten, doubled his fist,
and thumped the bull between the eyes.

The animal felt the blow and its knees buckled.
The farmer was right there when it happened
and watched the bull collapse.
Still holding his whip, he screamed blue murder!

A crowd gathered to watch the farmer's rage,
as he scraped his whip through the dirt.
The brother lifted his fists again, and the crowd
rallied to them.

It was self-defence, they chanted.
The bull was mad, a four-legged terrorist
that deserved what it got. The seconds grew hot
as the farmer's rage peaked.

They then saw the bull reviving, leg by leg;
until the farmer whipped it back to shape,
when the crowd dispersed,
the children were nowhere near.

WHAT SHOULD I CALL YOU?

I asked my father, what should I call you?
He answered, call me Dada.
I asked my grandmother, what should I call you?
She answered, call me Granny.
I asked my grandfather, what should I call you?
He answered, call me Mas Sam.
I wanted to ask my mother, what should I call you?
But she had left to buy sweets and never came back.

Years later, she returned holding a sweet
baby boy. I asked my mother, what should I call him?
She answered, call him Desmond.
My mother asked my father if she could put
Desmond to sleep on his bed. My father said, NO.
She sat in the doorway with Desmond sleeping on her lap.
I asked my mother, what should I call you?
She answered, don't wake the baby.

After she left that evening with Desmond on her hip.
I asked my father, what should I call my mother?
He answered, call her whatever feels right.
I asked my grandmother, what should I call my mother?
She answered, call her whatever sounds natural.
I asked my grandfather, what should I call my mother?
He replied, ask her, if you ever saw her again.

It took thirteen years before I saw my mother again.
I asked my father, are you sure she is coming?
He answered, that's what the letter said.
When my mother arrived
she sat down in the doorway, gazing up at me.
I asked my mother, what should I call you?
She answered, no, what should *I* call you?

CELIA SAID

Celia said duppies are real, so you stay there.
She said she always entered a graveyard at midday,
but she never goes inside her house without spinning around
three times, and never left a cooked pot on the stove
overnight, without sprinkling salt on the lid.

> Celia said the last time she was ever inside a graveyard
> at midday, she was picking guineps from a tree with her
> sister. She said she heard a loud crack and saw a tomb
> burst open. She said she saw smoke coming from
> the grave and a little white bird flying out of it.

Celia said she jumped out of the tree and ran, leaving her
sister still trying to fill her pockets with the guinep seeds.
Celia said her father believed in duppies and kept horseshoes
on both doors. She said he built a cross-shaped wooden stand in
the front yard, where he kept a glass filled with water and sage.

> Celia said her father taught her how to weed out duppies,
> how to beat a drum, and how to get into the holy spirit.
> She said she knew about parchment paper and how
> to sprinkle camphor water. She knew how to communicate
> with the dead and could speak the spirit language.

Celia said when walking at night, if you see a white sheet lying
across the road, don't step on it. She said you should carry a box
of matches to trick the duppies. She said you should
light two of the matches and pretend to light the third by scratching
the stick loudly on the box — that will surely confuse the ghosts.

Celia said her father took her to the graveyard at midnight and showed her how the dead rose. But when the sun rose, Celia said her heart felt heavy, and her mind was fuzzy. After three days of sprinkling camphor water on Celia, Celia said nothing. The doctor said Celia's mind had gone wandering. Her father said her mind was fine.

WINSTON

Winston
you know, it wasn't rude
you asking to move to Manchester
where you pictured the streets ripe with gold.

You sitting on dada's bed
fear quivering up your lips
waiting to hear the words
"he'll live…," you didn't.

His dreadlocks spread out like a black
cotton sheet spoiled by the stillness
of his wide eyes. Can you remember saying,
"I should a burned his thin body down to the bones"?

You sighing a breath of relief
when I said, "the police would get you."
Ms Vennetta coming close
telling me, "here is your father!"

I looked at you sitting on the rock,
your voice like dad's
"here is your father!"
It stayed with me for a long time.

Winston
I must tell you, England
is hard, nothing worth having is free.
No grave mourners or coconut trees.

No nesberry, star-apple, or sweet-sop,
nor yellow-tail fish boiling with
scotch-bonnet in a dutch-pot.
You would hate the beach-less streets

curse at the biting east wind and swear at the slow lazy
rain, you would despise daytime TV,
bin your bangers and mash
and pour a pound of salt on the toad in the hole.

Winston
I must tell you; it wasn't rude of you to ask.

AUNTIE LEE

While Auntie Lee knelt
under the weeping willow,
crying, her son waited on her verandah,
waving a cutlass at the sky.
He was talking to the fallen angel
he had met the day before.
The angel was sitting in his canoe
with a pot and a fire burning,
cooking a trunkfish
with ackee and quicksilver.
While the angel stirred the pot
with a three-pronged fork,
its moony-kitty eyes shone with the sun,
its hair moored the canoe to the clouds.
The angel poured from the cooking pot:
congo worms, maggots, and shooting stars,
then offered them to him to eat.
While Auntie Lee could not see the angel,
she could see her son's rage,
she could hear her son talking,
and watch him chopping at the air
until the cutlass chopped through
the windows and splintered the wood.
Auntie Lee took off her dress, pulled down
the straps on her underclothes,
and bore her breast.
Pulling on her curls, she scraped dirt
from the willow's root and rubbed it in her hair.
Lifting her eyes to the sky, she cried,
"Dis son you gimme, tek him back.
Tek him back to the hell him come from."

Her son, now choking on the angel's food,
did not hear his mother's
curse, but felt a sudden urge to run.
When Auntie Lee replaced her clothes
and rose to her feet, she did not see her son.
The verandah was empty and the windows
unbroken.
As Auntie Lee brushed the willow leaves
from her knees, she felt a kick inside
her womb and knew she was with child.

FIVE

MERMAIDS

Her grandmother said there were Mermaids living in the pond
by the post office.
She said she had seen them sitting on a large rock, combing
their long, wavy hair.
She said the Mermaids were holding back the sea from flooding
the entire town.
But, one day, the unwise town drunk went to court the Mermaids
and gave them a fright.
One dropped her golden comb as they dove into the blue pond
and swam out to sea.
The town drunk picked up the comb and took it home smiling,
obliviously.
On the third day, the sea climbed over the road and flooded
the shops and the streets.
She said the sea began to rage, throwing rough waves on land
for thirteen long nights.
On the fourteenth day, the town drunk's family escorted him
with the comb in hand.
He waded through water up to his waist back to the pond
to throw the comb in.
But as he leaned over, a fierce whirlpool began twirling,
the water thinning.
She said the family watched the drunk vanishing down, down
until he was gone.
No one went looking for him; they said it was expected,
a kind punishment.
To this day, when fishermen pull in their seines, they all throw
the biggest fish back.

THE BIRDMAN

He knew he wasn't like the parakeets
in the guinep tree or the egrets in the mangrove
or like the bridge where the river dirtied the sea, at breakwater.
He knew how to stay on the ground.

His rum cup in one hand, the other
pressed over his lips, he swayed on the piazza,
whistling through his fingers the bananaquit song. He had loved
a brown-skin wife who kissed him at the airport,

said she would see him in three months.
He rode the crowded bus home, his mind resting
on the empty sea. Eighteen years
passed, her kiss he still could remember. His fingers over his lips,

he honoured the birds, wishing to be
free, to be able to feel his wife's lips on his lips.
If he could he would soar to Canada and perch on her windowsill.
Chirping the bananaquit song,

hoping she would remember the green
fields of his love and the bridge above the mangrove bush
where the egrets sleep, where they made their first child.
After twenty-five years waiting.

His voice grew hoarse. The bananaquit song
faded. The shopkeeper placed a plaque,
the colour of parakeets, on the piazza wall,
which greeted the pink-edged eyes of his aged wife:

In fond memory of
The Birdman.

FIREFLIES

The moonless nights were golden.
A solitary dinner
candle flickering in its
bottle-labra and a host
of fireflies dancing in
the far shadows of the yard.

Us, not old enough to drink,
took sleeping pills to skip school
the next day. You sulked, mad
at the rising sun, vowing,
"tonite, we will tek double
than the frigging night before."

But at dusk, the fireflies
danced, blinking as you pulled me
toward the lane, a snake
trail, to watch for your father
while you leaned against the frame
of your lover's bicycle.

Months later, when the fireflies
faded, your lover drifted,
leaving you holding a silk
rope which your father detached
from the laden coconut
tree as your fingers trembled.

Then, when summer nights grew bright
with fireflies, you taught your
son their Island names, Peeny
Wally, Blinky Bug, Moony
Kitty – teaching him to be
even when the light dulled.

MOTHER SAID

X

It was not her shortcomings, mother said.
All this happened before you were born.
Our house was in a tenement yard
where the sun never goes. The walls were
blue. At night large toads came leaping
through the rooms, onto the beds, eating
food from the plates and besmirching the floor.
All this happened before you were born.

X

It was not her shortcomings, mother said
but your father had another wife
before us, and that hateful woman
paid an obeahman to take all my
new-born babies. Your father promised
to unfasten the curse by paying
the obeahman triple the fee.
All this happened before you were born.

x

It was not her shortcomings, mother said.
But the toads just kept coming until
we had to move address, but after
three days the toads found us, bringing black
flies with them and covering the ceilings.
Your father burned cow dung to drive them
out, but they rapidly multiplied.
All this happened before you were born.

x

It was not her shortcomings, mother said.
You were on your way. I was eight months
pregnant, soon due, but I grew skinny
losing weight, haunted by nightmares, and
falling over with vertigo, then
bedridden until the midwife's hands
delivered you at home that midday.
All this happened, and then you were born.

x

It was not her shortcomings, mother said.
But as the midwife placed you in my
arms, she mourned quietly for your health
while I wrote the name your father chose.
That night your daddy left the house
and returned with an empty suitcase.
He packed his belongings and left us.
All this happened the day you were born.

o

It was not her shortcomings, mother said.
The next day, at dusk, the toads and flies
did not come. I waited with thick nets
over your crib to claw at the curse.
Your father never came home, and you
strived beyond what was expected.
It was not her shortcomings, mother said.
But we had to save you when you were born.

LIMBO

Once a year, the old men in our town gathered in grandfather's yard,
beating basso drums.
Men talking, exchanging silent dialect that belonged to a world only the
old desire.

As the front lawn crowded with adults and children, we, future ones prac-
ticed our wake dance,
perfecting the limbo for the next grand event, when the drums are roused
again to mourn the dead.

Every beat played beneath the night sky on the old instruments is, to us, a
loss cry, a cold cue
that we are of this time, children born without links between our world
and the motherland.

As we dance to the basso drums, we hear our teachers' voices telling us,
forget, dance on the shadows of the past, make our dead proud. So, we bend,
trying not to let the sharp-talking rhythms in.

SIX

BIBLE AND KEY

I

That day was the worst. Can you remember
who took the money? I said it wasn't me,
you said you didn't find it fallen out anywhere,
your brothers said it wasn't them. We looked
everywhere.

II

Pearl began turning over the pages of the Bible.
Psalm twenty-three. The door key with the stem
placed in the middle of the psalm. She began tying
up the book. The steel bow sticking out. Can you
remember?

III

She said she needed two witnesses —
to help balance the Bible and key on their fingers.
Then X stepped forward and held out his index.
Can you remember hearing the words *by Saint
Peter?*

IV

Can you remember how the Bible began to turn
when they got to *by Saint Paul* and said your
brother's name? You running home calling for your
mother. We all know *the true and living God* never
lies.

V

Your brother wouldn't run. He said it wasn't him.
X got upset and said your brother was guilty. X
was on his way to the station when your mother
on the back of a bike, past him on her way to the
Obeahman.

VI

When your mother returned, she told the police
who had your brother kneeling on his shirt; the thief
was a light-skinned man with a crooked index finger.
The police said the *all-seeing* Obeah man knew his psalms.

VII

We glanced at X, and the police seized him and marched
him over to his bathhouse, a blue tarpaulined structure,
before leading him beside the still barrel waters,
the one place where everyone had forgotten to look.

A CALL TO DANCE

Inharmonious and dull, his voice was baritone, a deep
untamed rumble that echoed across the meadowed cow pasture.

Twice weekly, the warning strings of his Rhumba Box were heard
before the raspy sound of singing soared above the guango trees.

Then, Celia would come dancing in the field among the cows,
doing the Della Move, before displacing the butterflies.

She would skip around the grassy field with her long dress flying
around her ankles until she lost her balance or fell.

The cows would form a tight crowd gawking at her bending body
as she gyrated to the beat of her father's instrument.

We four would watch her from behind the boundary line, pointing,
laughing, agreeing that surely Celia was madwoman.

When the singing stopped, she would invite us four to play cartwheel
and line-less hopscotch, while the farmer rounds up the lowing cows.

But, one day, the strings plucked softly, and a voice angelic
and riveting travelled on smooth harmonics across the field.

Without thought, we four breached the barrier and began prancing
around the pasture, feeling unrestricted and unhampered.

We let out our hair and ran, frolicking, until the chanting
ceased, and the call of our parents echoed over the silence.

The singing started again, and we began unrooting our
hair and hanging strands of half-brown on the branches of the trees.

A cross was quickly tied together from sticks and itching vines
which we carried through the darkening fields to find Celia.

She was sat atop the Rhumba box wearing a crown of thorns,
her fingers softly plucking on the four strings of the old box.

The music stopped, and we four glanced around at one another,
surprised at the appearance of the other. We could not laugh.

Celia got up and pointed at us, one by one, then howled,
before hooting and convulsing, she then asked, who's laughing now?

THE WISEMAN

Mango season comes but once a year.
You must learn how to read its signs, my son,
by practising the mango season song,
which was taught to me by my own grandpa.

"May, you may get it.
June, it's due to you.
July, it's lying on the ground
but come August, it's all done."

Now that you know the mango song, my son,
you will never walk miles in the scorching sun
over hills, valleys, and bushlands
to only return with your two naked hands.

DONKEY RIDE

The lonely dirt lane that connected our house
to the graveyard was the donkey's land.
He owned it… an acre — from the ackee trees
to the first grey tombstone.

It was his Kingdom — his domain where none
but his master was allowed to go.
He would come charging… curbed by his rope
whenever we passed him.

Every midday, when he brayed loud in the shade
of the ackee trees, we'd pull our plaits
to make our hair grow as long as his breath
believing grandma's words.

Donkey ride was never far from our minds.
His master would send us to the shops
for cigarettes and once promised us a ride
on the froward donkey.

On returning, we called two lean boys to help
us on the donkey's back and fell off three
times roaring with laughter when we kept
sliding off his slick coat.

We commandeered him from his sanctuary
and took him beyond the hills for miles
into a forest of mango trees
laughing and racing him.

When the sun went west, it began to drizzle.
We tried turning the donkey around
but he ran further into the woods,
us slowly slipping free.

The rain drummed conspiratorially on plucked
leaves as we jumped from the feral mule,
watching him vanish with the thunder
encouraging him on.

We ran from the branches, afraid of lightning strikes.
Soaked to the bones, we returned home
one missing mule on our anxious minds.
At dusk, the tears ran free.

The next day, we met early, reciting our
lines — lies to tell the owner of his donkey's
plight when we heard loud braying coming
from the donkey's kingdom.

Running to the verandah, we saw him,
head thrown back and mouth turned towards
his master's house, with lips parted,
trying to turn us in.

MISCHIEF

I'm not going to tell you who poisoned the old
Tamarind tree. I'm not ready to disclose who was swinging from the
branch or what happened before they landed.
I'm not going to tell you about the empty fishing boat,
sinking. I'm not ready to tell you what happened to the shark that pulled
it in. I'm not going to tell you who tied the plastic around the shark's head,
or who started the fire under granny's bed.
I'm not ready to tell you who smoked the last cigarette, the tobacco,
and the seaweed from the cabinet. I'm not going to tell you who stole the money
from the letter, the mattress, and the savings can.
I'm not going to tell you who drank the Appleton rum,
then hid the bottle under the drum.
I'm not ready to disclose who muddied the white blankets on the wire,
drying. I'm not going to tell you who wore your favorite slipper,
or whose dog chewed up the leather strap.
I'm not going to tell you who set fire to the cat's tail
or who puts it out with a blanket from the trunk.
I'm not readying to disclose who ate both
jonnie-cakes and the four chicken legs,
for Uncle Sam's dinner.
I'm not going to tell you how I know all this.
don't ask me to squeal who done it!
No, I can't tell you about the match-sticks, the toxin
or the rope on the old fruit tree.
I can't tell you whose boat it was
or where the shark ended up.
I can't tell you about the rum, the weed
or who mixed in the mud.
I'm not going to tell you where I saw your English money,
spending. It wasn't your dog that bites through your slipper,
and I'm not going to tell you whose it was
because if I did, then it wouldn't be mischief.

MS

It was...
it was
her black dress
the charcoal headscarf, and the smell of rum drying on
her breath.

It was...
it was
her shadow less appearing at sunset whenever my granny
called, and the way her fingers tightened around
my hand.

It was...
it was
her bloodshot eyes and her tight dark lips as she squeezed
until my knuckles echoed inside
her palm.

It was...
it was
her shallow eyes and the way they watched mine for the guilty
tears she had expected me
to cry.

It was...
it was
her confidence that all children were liars and the snigger
of hearty indifference puffing her cheeks that had kept my
eyes hard.

It was…
it was
her thinning face and her
purple breath that taught me never to flinch, even when my hand
went numb.

HOT OIL

The knife was on the table,
Formica handle, brown
with a jagged blade
which she uses to scratch
the guts from the fish.

The sleepy oil burnt black
from chicken back fat
and plain flour Johnny cakes
coated in baking powder,
some bleak day last week.

The flat, round pan
that had lost its non-stick
base months before
is sitting wantonly on the top
of the white four-burner stove.

A girl sent by her grandmother
is about to make her debut attempt
at frying fish.
No instructions are given
only assumptions are implied.

She summons the blue flame
and sets the pan on top
then pours in the sluggish oil,
simultaneously dropping the fish in
before the fat has time to heat.

When all the fish are in the pan
the oil begins to sing, leaping
onto the cooker's top.
The girl now tries to turn the fish,
but they are breaking onto the fork.

She can hear her grandmother's
slippers echoing on the concrete
floor behind her.
She is trying to put the pieces together
before her grandmother reaches.

The older woman is staring
down at the pan, she grabs the fork
from her hand and begins scraping
the pan, scratching at the bottom
with restless vigour.

The girl cowers, and the fork
comes flying through the air
and bounces off the wall
above her head. She turns and runs
from the kitchen.

"Buy back me fish," her granny
shouts at the summit of her voice
but the girl keeps running
until she is far away from the kitchen
where she stays until the setting sun.

Her grandmother is waiting
on the veranda when she returns.
They both glance at each other
without mentioning the fish
or the years of unprovided teaching.

MY FATHER'S MOTHER

It wasn't
the
lowness
of the
cellar
or the
wooden
stilts the
house
stood on
that made
me
afraid
to crawl
under
and drag
the sick
puppies
out.
It wasn't
the way
the rocks
raked at my
knees when
I tried to bring
my legs
over
or the way
my head
bumped
against the

floorboards
when my
neck grew
tired.
It wasn't
the smell
of dirt
or the taste
of dog
on my
fingers
after.
It wasn't
these
ill-treatments
that made
me
hate my
father's
mother.
Instead
it was
the stick
she used to
make me
submit.

YES

In our uniforms, blue dress and white blouse,
we climbed the school wall
under the poinciana tree,
until we could see inside the station grounds.

I wasn't sure what we were looking for.
I had imagined we were going
to tease the prisoners again whose long
sorrowful faces stared out from behind their steel bars.

Your black shoes bent at their narrow points
as you gripped the wall.
Even after my hands grew
weak from clinging, you did not let go.

Knees scraping against the exposed concrete,
I rejoined you as our
schoolmates played
a sailor went to sea, sea, sea.

I followed your gaze to the see-through rooms
and saw what had taken
your attention, what had kept
you from our games of handball and skipping rope.

There, sitting on the mildewed floor, was your mother,
locked behind the irons of the cell.
Her blonde wig matted by her feet.
Her black eyeliner had streaked her painted cheeks.

An hour later, eating free bulgar for lunch,
you emptied your plastic plate
onto mine, got to your feet
and said, *what else is an unqualified woman in Negril to do!*

We linked arms and passed the stush girls whose fathers
owned hotels. They were drinking
Pepsi and eating buns with cheese.
I asked if you had always known about your mother, and you said *yes.*

SEVEN

GO TELL THE MOUNTAINS

Go tell it to the tall man who didn't care
one about your health, Georgette.

Go tell it to the young men who will care
and fear the killer in you, Georgette.

Go tell it to the Anglican priest, he cares
if your soul burns in hell, Georgette.

Go tell it to Jesus, see if He truly cares
about the sores on your legs, Georgette.

Go cry it to the doctor, he should care
more about your sex life, Georgette.

Go break it to your granny, she will care
about the shame it brings, Georgette.

Go tell it to your mother, she clearly cares
more about her rum bottle, Georgette.

Go spill it to your son, he shows he cares
about the days you have left, Georgette.

Go tell the mountains your fears and cares
but never lie to your conscience, Georgette.

THE SAME PSALM

Every week, when the Missionaries arrived
at the little house up the red-dirt lane,
the woman who said her name was Mary Magdalene
brought out her Bible and asked them to read the same Psalm.

She would order them to read Psalm 109 aloud,
to face her neighbour's house, where the sloping fence
was a perfect chamber pot post,
inspiring decades and decades of ingenious spite.

On one such visit,
the Missionaries suggested they read from a new psalm.
Psalm 23 was offered, but Mary was unyielding,
even when they asked if her name was really Mary Magdalene.

"I could tell you a lot that's not real in this town,"
she said and showed them her birth paper.
"But the Bible teaches us to love thy neighbours,"
they answered, after seeing that her name was as she had said.

"You could hardly call them thy neighbours," she answered,
"since I was married to the father,
and every time their pastor visits, he shouts the same Psalm,
that's how I know God hears not the prayers of the wicked."

The Missionaries left Mary Magdalene's house.
They knew their visits weren't bringing her any closer to God
so they decided to baptise her instead,
to dip her in the sea; that way, she could read the Psalm herself.

CELIA'S VISION I

The vision came to Celia
right there on the fallen tree.
She told the four something bad would happen
if they went up the hills that day.
But they had planned it all
and had even invited the prettiest girl on the street.

So, when Celia gripped the front of her blouse
they ignored her – poor, confused Celia.
She was trying to ruin their plans
to scare them into staying home and playing handball.
They ascended the hills, with Celia behind them
and walked until they reached the first mango tree.

But Celia began foaming at the mouth
and started to chant, "Turn back, turn back."
The four glanced up at the laden tree,
planning how to climb the branches.
When Celia's chanting got louder,
they made do with the ones already on the ground.

Seeing Celia's eyes turning white, then black,
the four decided to take the shortcut home.
Without warning, it began raining
the mango bags had begun weighing down
when two men appeared from around a bend.
They were wearing raincoats that bulged at the sides
and were walking only on the grassy embankment.

Celia whispered, gunmen, and they all froze.
They waited for the men to pass.
When the men reached them, one in red
asked the pretty girl for a mango
and said something about putting her on a cutting table,
which only Celia understood.

The pretty girl gave him the biggest mango
and when the men were out of earshot, Celia said, run.
The four and the pretty girl lightened their load
and began to run home, their mangos lying in the puddles.
Before long, a group of wet men dressed in police clothes
asked them to point in the direction the two men went.

Celia began foaming at the mouth again,
the vision had returned to her. The police waited.
They ordered the four to take the 'mother-woman' home
before setting off to hunt the fallen men.
Still in earshot, she pointed to the sky
and said, you will find them on the face of a cliff.

THE TADPOLES' POND

With a quart bottle of oil,
a rolled tissue for a wick,
you walk through the field,
shading the flame from the breeze.

You can hear the preacher's voice
over the hill, calling all
sinners to come to the pond
where the tadpoles swim.

From the top of the hill, you
see a long white tent, sparkling
and hear the preacher singing:
all wrong doers come,

come on down to the pond where
the tadpoles swim and forsake
the old you, your old ways, till
your burdens grow light.

You blow out the lesser lamp
and run to the bigger glow
till you reach the tent. Sinners
kneeling on their knees.

The preacher rests his hand on
your pendent head and tells you
to be free of all evil.
Free your mind and heart

from all principalities.
You wait at the side and watch
the saints speaking in new tongues,
jerking and ticking.

One comes to you carrying
a tadpole in a clear jar.
She whispers, what would you gain
if Christ comes tonight

and you are here left behind?
She gives you the jar and tells
you to follow the sinners,
down into the pond.

But you are scared now, holding
your jar, watching your tadpole
swim, observing the sinners
getting in the pond

and wading up to their waist.
They freed their tadpoles, their tails
fanning next to legs, kicking
back into the past.

They are creating a new
them. But you know that you could
never return to that life
to be born again.

You turn to leave as the new
saints crawl from the lake
into a new life, afraid
to expose the sin

festering on your brown legs.
You watch to see their changed forms
knowing your last way to life
is through these waters.

NOSTALGIA

I'm being called back to my childhood.
To the dirt road fading into the marled hill
to the place where the steel drums
grew out of the red clay. Where the yam
vines became skipping ropes and cottas for our heads.

I'm being summoned back to the bush
where the mangos are worth the five-mile
walk in the heat and the fear of cows
sending us back through the field over
the stone wall that ends where our eyes cannot reach.

I'm being demanded back to the beach,
the pears, the bulla-cakes, the soft drink
bottles selling for a dollar, and the hand--
balls, the cricket in the front yard
and the fights — the fights I will always win.

I'm being given back to you, to the land
of my birth, to the childhood of my past
to the mother, father, and the sisters
who longed to say, "Sit, me we plait you hair."
I'm being handed back to you — my childhood home.

THE MUSIC

On the grand front lawn of Ms. Bessie's house.
For one day every summer, Children
from every corner of Red Ground
were mesmerised by the music's melodies
and would find themselves on the lawn
blowing iridescent bubbles.
drinking English lemonade and chasing balloons
drifting around the yard.

They knew her only as Ms. Bessie,
a senior Jamaican living abroad,
who would return every summer
with barrels of sweets, second-hand clothes,
barbies for girls and tractors for boys.
The music would play until late into the evening
with children dancing, hula hooping,
eating liquorice and peanut butter sandwiches
until it was time to leave, optimistic for next year.

But as the years slipped by,
the front lawn of Ms. Bessie's house
grew into a meadow of wildflowers and weeds.
The path leading to the veranda
had relinquished itself to burr-bush and mongoose.
The children, now much older,
would cut the lawn to the beat of machetes
and hand out hard sweets to the youngsters passing by.

What happened to Ms. Bessie?
They gathered to ask the new occupant,
who shook his head and narrowed his eyes.
Then, a different music began to play.
The type that brought adults queuing for hallucinogens
and shook the pillars of the community.
Soon, the music started to speak to Ms. Bessie's children
for Red Ground had become a town of dead dreams.

LADY OWL

She remained the patoo in the pear tree,
across the wire fence, in the pasture lands,
at the back of our house. She was hooting
again, calling out late at night.
Lady Owl, our nocturnal priestess,
would visit once a year,
dressed in white turban and a pencil
tucked behind her ear.
She would mutter as she scratched lines
on the kitchen floor, clearing
the house by lamplight of evil spirits, duppies,
and demons. She was our patoo aunt, lady Alga, with the deep
round eyes, great for spotting lizards, spiders,
and the supernatural.
She said she had the gift of sight,
the ability to see at an angle no one else could.
To prove her point, she would spin herself
twice round in her loose frock,
wheeling her body with her arms pinned
tight at her sides. As children, we would wake
to find her marching through our bedroom,
carrying her *Home Sweet Home* lamp
and hooting the name of the person
she said would die in a fortnight.
The next day, the dogs would begin
their ritual digging in the flowerbeds,
while Johncrows circled above the chosen house.
When two weeks passed and the funeral
did come, we children learned to mark her words.
On her last visit, she rushed through the hall
in her long flowing dress,

growling and raising her arms, tapping
on the low board ceiling.
Her brother's name was on her lips: *Coolie-man.*
She said she had seen his name in the book of life,
that he had come to her bedside that night
and roused her from her midnight dream.
Our father, eyes still heavy with sleep,
took her by the hand and told her their brother
had died the year before, that she had predicted
the sea would take him almost a year
to that night. But she hooted *Coolie-man*
through clenched teeth until we all
went back to sleep.
When daylight came our lady owl had disappeared,
leaving her headscarf behind like a shroud
airing on the bamboo chair.

MICHAEL

He came when the sun was still setting.
His long fingers gripping the steering
of his wooden handcart as its four rubber
wheels crept over the hill. He had brought
with him his jerk chicken drum and an empty

bag with room for leaving. His large bloodshot
eyes were kind, so when he offered to pay
our grandmother for a night's bed,
he left his cart and drum by the front door
and marched across the hall to the spare room.

When daylight came, we found a pudding
pan stacked with chicken foot and gizzards
sunning on the lawn. He must have spent the night
cleaning the birds he brought tucked in his cart
with his ten-inch knife.

Around midday, his hands were red with spice
from rubbing paprika into the meat.
He unpacked the coals and arranged the meat
on the grill. At dusk, he pushed his cart back down
the hill. We didn't think we would see him again.

At half-past three, in the early hours, he had returned
knocking on the windows. Our grandmother opened
the door, and he came in looking disappointed
his chicken was still in the drum, and he had used
up all his money on supplies.

She showed him back to the spare room and told him, 'people in Negril only eat from those
they know. But with time, everyone will know who you is.' That morning, he fed us the meat with fried rice for breakfast then for lunch and told us he was considering pimping.

EIGHT

CARRYING WATER

At dawn, when the grey night has lifted
its veil, she would rise, white bucket in hand
and red shawl around her shoulders,
which would become kata for her head.

A small queue of people lined the backyard
of the three sleeping brothers —
one wise and two foolish. When it was her turn
to bleed the tap,

she would rest her bucket on a dusty block
and use her developing knee
to keep the container still. Then a door,
part-charred would rattle

as the water swells toward the top of the bucket.
She kept her eyes on the shaking door handle
until the wise brother in a smoke-stained vest
was standing on the threshold of the door.

The queue said, 'Morning' simultaneously.
She froze with the crowd in silence,
waiting for him to check their faces and give them
the nod of approval before anyone could relax.

Once her bucket was full, she picked up her kata,
rolled her red shawl into a flat mat, and placed
it onto her head. She then heaved the bucket
onto her right knee before lifting it onto her head.

The crowd watched without interrupting
as she balanced the bucket, which shook
unsteadily on the kata before settling.
She left the wise brother watching the pipe.

She passed the front of the three brothers'
house, now a charred ruin, which was once
a lovely home until that December night
when a fire gnawed through the entire building,

leaving only the wise brother's room standing.
She remembered seeing firefighters blasting
the engulfed building. And all that wasted water
would take the brothers years to recompense.

We had been preparing for the worst. But still, there was an excitement we could not deny. Our first hurricane. Mummy had brought all the candles she could afford in the shop. She stacked the fridge with corned beef and cans of tinned mackerel. She tied the matches and the rest of the dry goods in plastic bags. We shut the extra batteries in a white keg. She then sent us out to buy kerosene oil for the lamps. We didn't think of storing water. We knew plenty of that was coming. Instead, we tied up our good clothes in black bags and stuffed them in the barrel. The TV and video player were covered with large plastic sheets.

All this time, Dada was still at work. He was helping to batten down his boss' roof. When he came home, we handed him his hammer a tin of nails, and hoisted slabs of board up to him on our roof. The power was still on. The radio was playing. The hurricane was still heading for our Island. When the rain came, the wind followed shortly after. We played cards and jacks in the back bedroom. Mummy was in the kitchen trying to cook the dinner.

Dada was rushing around the rooms, checking for leaks. The wind grew stronger. We could see it on the almond tree. The limbs were breaking, threatening to fall onto the verandah. Dada wanted to go out with his machete to chop it down. Mummy wouldn't let him. We wouldn't let him. Then from our window, we saw our neighbour's roof flying past. It landed on another house and shifted that house. The neighbour came knocking on our door, crying. She was standing in water up to her knees. She was so old; we let her in. Our roof then began to disappear. First the slabs, then the nails, and then the zinc. Dada wanted us to evacuate. But mummy had shared the dinner. No one wanted to eat. Mummy did not want the food to go to waste. She covered the plates and left them on the stove. The old lady was wrapped under a blanket. Dada left with her in the rain. They hurried with their heads down. They were running for the Church. It was only six hundred yards from our house. Mummy told us to get dressed. Dada came back. He told us to wait. He then left with mummy. But we left the house together. Dressed in nothing but our t-shirts and shorts, we ran out into the wind, into the stinging rain.

THE CRAB-CATCHERS

Popping torchlight brought
the children and their rippling shadows
to the morass where the bush-crabs
rested at the mangrove's edge:

Crabs up to their bellies in mud,
seated by their doors. With giant claws
pillowed on sludge, their dotted eyes
watched shadows passing before the moon.

Each child, armed with crocus-bags
and bottles of light looked like fireflies
caught in the thickets in the night,
with mosquitos playing Jonkonnu on fifes.

The crabs, seeing the darkness exploding
with light, turned away from the moon.
They scrambled on their stiletto legs
and dashed down their watery holes.

Stretching and reaching
through the escapees' doors, with bare hands
the children brought the crabs back
to face the knots in the burlap bags.

Now tip-toeing on their neighbours' carapaces,
they foam and watch the sky from the bottom
of a drum, waiting for a cloud to stand still
before the mongoose sun.

CELIA'S VISION II

One was pulled from the sea
and discarded in the police courtyard.

The other, maybe a fugitive
clinging to a lifeboat for Cuba or worse.

Three days before, Celia had seen them,
skittish, fleeing the police handcuffs.

One had paid the ultimate price,
jumping from Negril's unfamiliar cliffs.

His body was left on display for hours
with the town stopping to shake its head.

All who saw the corpse that day
said *Negril was safe. It was impassable,*

our police force is fearless
and our town is protected by a hungry sea.

Let all intrepid and boldface bad men beware
for Negril is where the antics end.

The young boys in the crowd laughed,
and left the courtyard first.

Celia watched them without speaking,
she knew with them – the next generation,

who knew the cliffs like their backyard,
Negril's peaceful days were numbered.

THE FROG AT NIGHT

Sitting on a powdery ground, slowly
soaking out the green banana stains.
A metal tub is filled with clothes up to its brim.

The force of each hand squeezes the suds
over the edge, spilling the smell of blue soap
and Clorox bleach, as each

garment is submerged below the surface
of milky water, changed by cubes
of Reckitt's Crown Blue.

Then came the sound of washing:
"scrups, scrups." The non-flexible
whites were left overnight to soften up.

Steadily beneath the moonlight,
under the banana trees, the water
stagnated until a speckled frog leaping

past plopped in by curiosity and sat still
on the raft of clothes like on lily-pods
until its lycra began to strip

clean from its freckled body. As the cloud
shadowed the moonlight, it hopped off
into the fields, trying to shake the heat

of the tub. In the morning, its thin pigments
floated above the clothes, colouring
each garment with spotted fragments.

WHEN DOGS DREAM

When dogs dream in Jamaica, what do they dream of?
An Island where dogs are treated with respect and one love.
An Island where motorists allow dogs to cross without hazard.
An Island where dogs are taught to fetch instead of flinch.
An Island where dogs are fed at least one good meal a day.

When dogs dream in Jamaica, what do they dream of?
An Island where their masters eat three meals a day.
An Island where their masters work five days a week.
An Island where education is free.
An Island where dogs are seen as friendly, not ferocious.

When dogs dream in Jamaica, what do they dream of?
An Island where the history of dog savagery is forgotten.
An Island where dogs are no longer taught to fight or bite.
An Island where dogs are seen as intelligent beings.
An Island where dogs are treated as part of the family.

When dogs dream in Jamaica, what do they dream of?

NINE

CARNIVOROUS

Let's talk about Uncle Ben,
who stood at five-foot-ten,
with a prickly white beard
and chest as broad as washing board.
He had an offensive wife
and a milk occupation most of his life.
His home was near Antarctica
but he preferred it in Jamaica
where the children are friendly
and the penal laws are scanty.
He visited once a year
with a fan to move the air
and whenever you were bending
you could feel a draught rotating.
He kept a bag of sweets
which he buried beneath the sheets,
and told the girls to hunt
while his hands restrict and stunt.
But his wife caught him peeping
beneath a girl's dress reaching
only then could the girls relax
when she gave him the judicial axe.

PAPER KITE

When you are a child, you think you will
never die, not until you see someone like you
lying in a small white casket
and you are standing there next to a mother,
watching her cry, thinking that if a child
aged eight could die, then so could I.

A small crowd had gathered on wet soil,
with the sun going down behind the locust tree.
The singing grew as Lamar's casket was lowered
into a half-hole. A girl, aged five, was thrown
across the grave three times. Her father was afraid
that she, too, might die if Lamar's ghost

could not learn to forget his past and the living.
I, too, wanted to be thrown across the grave, but no
one thought it was necessary, or perhaps they knew
Lamar did not need me as much as I thought he did.
The crowd stayed until the casket was sealed in
before leaving him to rest

with the older dead. I walked in between the rows
of guinep trees, hoping that if I was to go
to the shops that night, that I would not smell the fresh
ointment on his skin or see him crossing the lane back
to his mother, back to his little room where the tail
of his paper kite still flutters in the wind.

THE SWIVEL CHAIR

The old lady had once had a daughter who died
in New York. Her body was shipped home and buried
under a jackfruit tree. Her apartment stripped
and a swivel chair sent across the Caribbean Sea.
The chair arrived on a Friday in a large brown box.
The old lady loved the chair because it showed
the life her daughter had. She placed the chair
on the verandah next to her wicker bench.
All summer, the chair on its metal column
turned and turned and turned. The old lady feared
that the chair would cease to be
a swivel chair if the turning did not stop.
In the heat of the sun, the chair turned and turned
and turned. Its molasses-coloured oil seeped up
from its base as the chair turned and turned.
The neighbours who came to the old lady's house
watched the chair turn right round, then left, and right
round again. The old lady was kind, and the local children
enjoyed sitting on her verandah eating mangoes
and singing ring-game songs.
The children also liked spinning on the foreign chair:
never had they seen a chair that goes round and round
like a merry-go-round. The old lady knew that the chair
would not last if the turning did not stop and would
ask the children not to spin as much. But the children would
not listen. Each day, they'd come to the old lady's verandah
and whirl and whirl on the swivel chair, laughing, whooping,
and singing. They did not know what the chair meant.
The old lady did not tell them that the chair had belonged to
her only daughter. Instead, she would ask them
not to spin as much, but the swivel chair turned

and turned until one day,
the old lady's soft voice faltered. She did not ask the children
to stop as she had done before. She watched them turn
and turn the memory of her child into creaks and oil.
And each day, the children came and sat down
in pairs singing dirty bus, dirty bus, round and round,
donkey want water, wash him down.
As the sun was setting behind the sea,
the chair began to squeak and squeak as if
the voice of her dead daughter was calling from within
the leather seat. The children heard the squeak
but kept on spinning and spinning and spinning.
The old lady watched in silence as the metal column
grew longer and longer. It rose up until she could see its
metal tip sharp. The seat tumbled to the floor.
The children were still clinging on when it crashed
to the ground. They squealed and laughed
and giggled. The children tried to push the column back
inside the base but could not. They drifted off,
leaving the chair in halves. The old lady watched the children go
one by one. She looked at the broken chair and thought
of her daughter's voice and the children's song
and felt something swells inside her heart. She called her son
to take the base and the seat to the back room and lock them in
with the bed-foot and frame of her daughter's things.
Whenever the old lady passed by the door, she could hear
the children's song haunting the room. At night when she could
not sleep, she would hear her daughter's voice singing
in a foreign accent: dirty bus, dirty bus, round and round,
donkey wants water, wash him down.

BLIND SPOT

We heard him on the radio
choking the frequency, clairvoyant,
psychic reading on air.

A cataclysmic tremor
will overpower you in a crowded
place, he warned a listener.

A fainting fit will overwhelm
your consciousness and occupy your mind.
Avoid marketplaces.

His popularity took root.
A true prophet, seer, visionary,
people's fortune-bringer.

Then, there he was in the flesh. Real,
and gazing through a telescope at the sun,
from his false veranda.

Our car divided the queue,
young men paying to know what grand future
lied in the sun for them.

From Auntie's crystal balcony,
we watched the crowd amass. See dat trickster?
She asked us; him won't last.

We kept visual, observing
the seekers face for signs of discontent
as they descended, hushed.

We read it in the News Papers,
a shocking tale, psychic, fortune-teller
found dead a mile from home.

They played him on the radio
one last time, as listeners said goodbye,
his words heavy with lies.

NINE-NIGHT

Ena had laid out her black dress and stockings
on the bed to let the creases uncrease
and selected her fan for the service in the Anglican
Church Hall.

The Wake singers were scratching on their graters,
playing pot-cover-heads and beating their drums
while the crowd danced and sang:
Roll Jordan Roll.

Her daughter's body had been brought home from Canada
by her four children. It was the night before her
funeral. Ena sat on the verandah gazing
at the festivity,

aware that Royston, her eldest son, had taken his sister's death
to heart and was laid up in bed, breathing heavily.
She knocked the ashes from her billiard pipe
and listened with her hands

on her lap, to the hired voices singing. Come tomorrow,
she knew their songs would turn hers to tears. Ena
saw the darkened sky above the crowd
flash with streaks of lightning.

The Mento band stopped beating. A cloud of smoke
from a brick fire drifted over the crowd.
She saw men running towards the back of the house
carrying buckets filled with melted ice.

The drum cooking the curry goat was on fire.
Royston had got up to use the bathroom,
when the smoke floated through the glass panes,
and fogged the room.

Ena's youngest son came and stood in the doorway
looking down at her in her wicker chair. His breath
fumed with overproof when he said, "You not going
to look at you son? The fucker's in there dying?"

She got up without rebuking him and hurried
to the back room. Royston was placed on her bed,
face cotton coloured. He was laid out next to the dress
she would wear in the morning, then nine days after.

Ena took a bucket of water and sponged his feet.
She ordered the band to play, but the rain
had begun to descend. They waited as the rain
and thunder drummed on the zinc roof.

TEN

HOWARD'S OARS

He was ruled by the full grey moon
the fourth son of Maroon and German blood.
Eyes deep blue, his hands inured
to pulling daily seines to canoes,
until noon.

He was divided by a malignant star
the only child to be born of the lunar touch.
Once a year, he would vanish into the coral
wilderness of his spurious mind,
and its swelling scar.

He would lay siege in the oarless zinc kitchen -
in his barracuda's den, where he scaled his nephew's
flesh with his swordfish's blade. Like a noxious
eel drowned by a kerosene fire,
his mind was let back in.

He would have no memory of the day before
and would sit beneath his yellow door and tells
the story of a giant fish with stings and wings
and moonshine eyes, which stole
his oars and watched him die.

MAN TO MADMAN

He was a man until he became a madman,
a haunting-the-streets type with no diagnosis,
pacifier, or protection, except for his family name.

We would see him salivating at the side of the road,
shirtless, muscular, hair matted, back bending
as he tossed his head from side to side, shouting,

"COH!"

True, he was an unchained hazard, berserker
the kind of crazy we did not want to meet in the streets
alone, but whenever we did, we knew to flee from sight.

The new young men said they were brave enough
to face him, to stand their ground, to haul and pull him.
But those who tried found themselves dodging boulders,

"COH!"

Then, we were squatting under a poinciana tree
playing, heaping the red blossoms covering the ground
when my friend let out a whispered scream.
I glanced up and saw him standing over us,
holding a plank above his head.
A voice from within said, don't run. Just ignore him.

"COH!"

So, we looked away and heard him wandering off.
When we asked our granny why he had left us alone?
She answered *because you treated him like a man.*

THE PUMP HOUSE

We all knew the pump house stunk in August.
For four weeks, we would ingest its gastric
stench whenever we pass the large houses
near the stagnated concrete vats.

On their way home from work, our fathers would
curse the air and shout the name of the pump
operator, imploring him to turn
the tattered engine manually.

He would offer up the same sacred words,
'Let the rich inhale their own carnal stink.'
Come the end of August, the smell would lift,
leaving the clean air soiled with suspicions.

I, Celia, witch, mother-woman, obeah-worker
yet, none a that is really who I am.
My father's granny was a witch, true, true,
from Scotland she came outta Macbeth's cave/
castle/château... halleluiah! All houses, true, true.

She landed at Bloody Bay Beach, and ordered workers
to build her a castle outta fishbones.
She was Lady of the wattle-stick hut,
rain-drenched and lean, with fingers knotting up
her dress when Greatpa met her, she called him Malcolm.

Him rooms grew small as she bulged on butter and bread
and amused him with tales of knights and blights,
and violent spells, fake deaths, and rough seas.
Their wedding night, Greatpa saw her skinless
and stepping from the window ledge onto hungry air.

Him grabbed the arrowroot goo and wiped it on the frame
before hiding underneath the table,
watching until first dawn for her return.
When she came through the window, red and sleeked
she took her skin from a box; whispered, skin, fit, it's me.

Soon, more hell broke loose when well children started dying.
Greatpa tried to contain her might again
but she wailed that no man can hold her down
if a king couldn't keep her from her will
then, no farmhand with no true power could tame her.

She ran from the house that bright night and never came back.
Greatpa went up and down looking for her,
and called himself King Malcolm of Scotland,
my grandmother was Lady Suzanna
and my father, Lord Herman of Red Ground, of Scot's blood.

So, I am more than what people say, yes, yes, I am
a daughter of greatness, of queens and kings.
My bloodline can be traced back to monarchs
power, beauty and great divinity.
Call me no witch or mother-woman. Call me power.

IF ME DID KNOW

I didn't know what possessed me
to take the seat of a stranger.

I was on a plane from Montego Bay
when a woman asked

me to exchange seats. I am a good
Jamaican, so I did.

When the plane stopped in London
a man in white shirt

with a pen in him pocket escort me
through a back gate.

"you didn't eat your meal," him say.
"So you must be a drug

mule!" A drug-mule? Is what him say
to me? I am a forty-nine

year old woman, from the gully. The
only mule I know was

Maas Allen's old donkey, who had one
good foot and a chewed

off ear. Him showed me to a doctor's
bed and told me to let down

me hair. To take off me clothes,
to show me-self like pickney

chasing fresh air. When me holler "after
me no done noting!"

him left him chair and came back with a
woman. "Is your name

Wendy Martin?" I told them it wasn't.
She opened my passbook,

saw Tanya Weir. "You're saying you're
not Martin?" "Is that me say

is hear you can't hear?" We went on
like this till the tea them

bring was a cup of ice. And me start
to forget why me board

the blue and white bird, in the first
place. The woman gave

me back me clothes and told me to
enjoy my stay. I could

a cut me eyes on her, but I couldn't
wait. I saw me brother standing

far away, him mobile phone to him ear.
Him waved, came running over.

I couldn't look him in the face or tell
him why me was so, so late.

ACKNOWLEDGEMENTS

A small percentage of these poems has appeared in *PN Review*, *bath magg*, Carcanet's *New Poetries VIII*, *Wild Court*, *RTÉ Radio 1 The Poetry Programme*, *Exacteditions* and *The Tangerine*.

I thank my editor, John McAuliffe, for his patience, careful eye and indefatigable guidance.

Special thanks to Scott Thurston at The University of Salford for pointing me in the right direction when I was looking for a clear path and for not being afraid to say, *try again*.

Thanks to Michael Schmidt for being Michael Schmidt, and credit to the exquisite creative team at Carcanet.

Thanks to my mother for allowing me to find inspiration in the shadows of the past.

To my father, Errol Herman Walker, who is no longer with us and to my brother, Winston Washington Walker, who went missing in June 2020...

Special thanks to my friends: Max Behr, Julia Crawford, Dympna Edwin, Tahira Hussain, Rachael Hadfield, Delsie Martin, Vicki Leng, Keziah Paul, Nickeisha Vickers and Devon Walker, without whose love and support this book would not have been possible.

My sincere gratitude to Joel and Jasmine Walker for allowing me the time and space to write.